Deluxe
BOX of CRAYONS

Donna,
For all the lovely
things you've brought
into my life - turtles
and beautiful beaches
and smiles!
Thank you, dear!
Kathy 3/28/12

Deluxe
BOX of CRAYONS

Poetry & Collage
Kathy Lohrum Cotton

Chaplain Publishing
Lubbock, Texas

Deluxe Box of Crayons
Copyright © 2012 by Kathy Lohrum Cotton

All rights reserved. Published by Chaplain Publishing
3104 County Road 7520, Lubbock, Texas 79423

Some poems have appeared previously in *Mind Dances, Living Communique, Shawnee Hills Review, The Writer's Voice, Poet's Post, Distilled Lives, Voices on the Wind,* and illinoispoets.

Digital collages include images from: Broderbund's The Print Shop 23.1, © 2002-2008, HMH Consumer Company Limited, and its licensors, all rights reserved; Photography by Keith Cotton (pages 3, 20, 59, 64, 83, 88, 89), used by permission; photographs and digital artwork by the author; and family snapshots.

Book design and cover by Kathy Lohrum Cotton

ISBN 978-0-9847362-2-5

Library of Congress Control Number: 2012930417

Printed in the United States of America

*To all who have loved a poem
or loved a poet.*

CONTENTS *Illustration*

CONTENTS *Poetry*

WILD COLORS, 2011. WORD PAINT, 2011. WILD RIDE, 2011.

My Colors

WILD COLORS, 2011.

2

On the Loom

The warp of me
is Quaker gray,
a quiet woolen thread—
modest, utilitarian,
looped simply
on my frame.

But, oh, the weft,
the vibrant weft of me,
weaves in and out
those sturdy strands
with shocking shades of
peacock and cockatoo and
shimmery hummingbird.

Co-mingled:
the whisper
and shout of my life.

KATHY, SPIRAL STAIRS, 2009.

3

Extravagant Color

This is the paint dripping
from my brush

petals of poppy

mandarin peel
and lemon zest

velvet moss from
damp woodlands

peacock feathers
with piercing eyes

dark-wash denim
concord grapes
newborn lilacs

white light enfolding
its full spectrum

Eager bristles soak up exquisite
pigment and fragrance and texture

from eighteen decillion
red–yellow–blue views

splash them lavishly
across empty-canvas days

drenching the simplest
moment in extravagance

never a need
to contemplate
scarcity

redorangeyellowgreenblueindigoviolet

Deluxe Box of Crayons

BENEATH PLAIN SKIN, 2011.

Beneath this pale Caucasian skin—
the skin of my mother's mother and father's father,
beneath this unremarkable brown hair
and behind these ordinary brown eyes
that are the eyes of all my family, even the dog,

beneath, behind, beyond this mundane commonness, I am

the Deluxe Box of Crayons: one-hundred-twenty unblended colors
scribbling exotic names—Cerulean, Burnt Sienna,
Mahogany, Maize, a crowd of immigrant pigments
unwilling to melt in my melting pot.

This Deluxe Box holds Fuchsia to attract hummingbirds.
Quaker gray for silent sitting. Outrageous Orange for
stumbling over politics. In the company of Blue, I can

match that patch of sky, her silk shirt, his denim jeans.
See me here, fiery Red as habanero; there—White as arctic ice.

Some believe I should defect from every hue but one,
become a solitary color's citizen, wear a single country's seal.

But I am the Deluxe Box, dressing my heart in tie-dye,
rainbows, confetti; waving on the hill of each moment
its hand-made, one-of-a-kind flag. I am the Deluxe Box

whose skin is red and yellow, black and white,
male and female, flower and beast, bright light and midnight.

Come close, look inside. Watch me search
my chameleon stash for a deluxe handful of myself
perfectly matched to you.

I am the Deluxe Box of Crayons.

RED MEMORY, 2011.

8

waiting for me,
wearing a red dress

Red Dress

For this anniversary I planned to bring you flowers:
a bouquet of favorite red roses to cascade
over our names, carved side by side above our wedding date

and flanked by digits of beginnings, endings—
my birth date followed by a tentative dash.
Yours, by finality.

But this year I bought no saddle of silks
to ride on the time-galloping back of black polished granite.

Instead I drifted from flower shop to dress shop,
where I bought this red sheath, hung incongruently now
with a row of jeans—an anniversary dress to decorate my closet,
a remembrance of your unfaded whisper:

I knew I was in love with you when you were eighteen.
I saw you sitting on the swing,
waiting for me, wearing a red dress.

GENE COTTON, 6.12.44—3.23.01

ROSE DANCE, 2010.

Imaginary Meaning

On a polished casket
or diva runway. In a
well-tended garden
or the hand
of another woman

unfolding crimson holds
imaginary meanings
of a moment.

Only to an untrained
child is the rose

simply
a red
flower.

In the Seed

I yam what I yam. . . .
—POPEYE, 1933

In its beginning,
the scant millimeter
of the poppy seed

holds the coming root
and stem, green leaf,
red petal. And I,

beginning to end,
am who I am in my
scripted kernel. But

the roll of the dice is this:
where the seed falls. Who
would I be, planted in
Chile or China,
Iceland, Zimbabwe?

Still me: brown-eyed,
pale-skinned,
X-chromosomed. Still prone

to love words and symmetry
and red. The same little flower,
tossed by some other
wild wind.

GREEN SPROUT, 2011.

12

Interior Landscapes

Thoughts shift from deep forest to fenced-in yard,
from meandering paths to incessant traffic,

a thousand greens to lean wordscapes
sorted by height and hue.

I sweep a poor plot of ideas, paved with
low-maintenance concrete, edged by boxwood

and fragments of color in plastic pots,
far from the wildflower carpet of a rich rotted floor.

But sprouts with ancient roots crack my packed surface,
call me to come to my senses, trample the fences I built.

Just below the drone of my constant weeding, I hear
wriggling whispers: sacred vines untangling,

acorns pressing into trees, dead words decomposing
along fresh-water streams. The wholeness of life

welcomes me home.

sprouts with ancient roots
crack my packed surface

SALT AND PEPPER PLAY, 2011. SUPER MOON, 2011. THREADS, 2010.

Grayscale

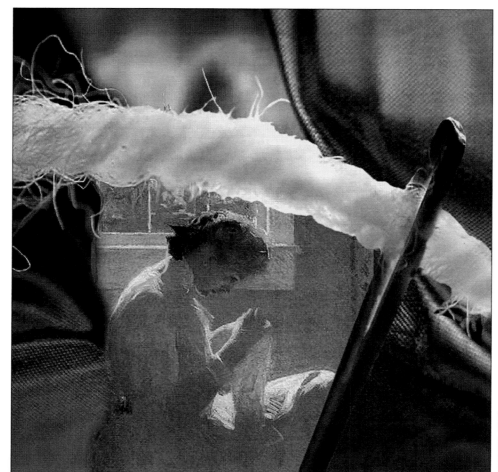

THREADS, 2010.

16

Diversities of Gray

My eyes scissor down
this bolt of asphalt
with its dingy white selvage

unfolding toward a band
of silver crepe sky,
pressed thin beneath layers
of pearled sateen,
somber business flannel,
slate and charcoal wools.

Utility poles, like old needles
with drab thread,
push even stitches
along the highway's edge.

Content without extremes
of black and white,
I wrap myself
in the soft comfort
of an overcast day.

Soft Angora Sweater

The world sees you
wearing this dull gray pain
close to your skin—a thin,

tight layer of mail armor
that tortures every move,
repels all who come near.

But luckily, Love is blind
and adept at translating
rough-surfaced braille.

She can wrap herself
around you like
a soft angora sweater,

pastel warmth
a perfect fit
for the healing heart.

SEASONING, 2010.

18

Salt and Pepper

There was a time
when I would shake out
the bottled-up memories
of conversation
like salt and pepper
sprinkled onto a plate.

I might sit at the kitchen table
and play with my monochrome
versions of spoken words
the way a child plays with food—
hiding a pile of peas beneath
macaroni, leapfrogging
stray kernels of corn.

But more often this word work
was sleuthing with magnifying glass
and tweezers, a serious sorting
into pulverized piles—
crystalline intentions here,
dark specks of regret there.

Now, I leave the shakers
on a shelf,

Close the cupboard doors.
Walk away.

After all, words are never simply
black and white.

They tumble out,
nicked and scraped by
tooth or tongue,
undercoats transformed
in catalyst
of eye and ear,

rehearsed, rebirthed
to live new lives.

Words are never
simply
black & white.

I am never
simply
black and white.

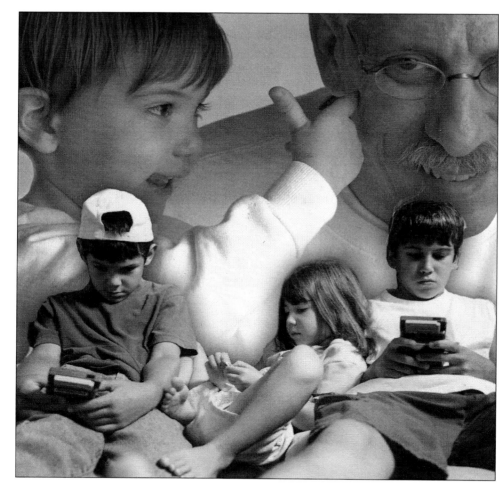

LEFT, POWER OF TOUCH, 2011.   RIGHT, TINY EMPTINESS, 2011.

Without Touch

Between pigment-on-plaster
fingertips of God and man,
Michelangelo left
a tiny emptiness,
the Ancient's index poised
near the hopeful nail bed
of full-blown incompleteness.

Without touch,
what is there?

The hand of the Creator
stretching across the Sistine ceiling
to *almost* give Adam life,

the not-quite-suckled child,
could-have-been comforted friend,
longing lovers in separate rooms—

all of us, reaching across our tiny
emptiness for caress and clasp,
holding and being held,
for completeness
that meets us in touch

Passing People

Because there was us once,
there can never be
the same you
or the same me again.

It's not the touch
of a fairy wand
that changes things.

It's the touch
of passing people.

LEFT, DREAM STORIES, 2008.

Mining Inspiration

Descend the inspiration shaft, wearing steel-toed Wellingtons,
lamp-lit helmet, riveted denim. Alongside your worn pick-axe

carry a caged-canary alarm and a snapping tin packed
with little sandwiches. Watch the head-light beam

its traveling circle on ancient compressed walls of words,
on deep veins plunging farther, farther down thesaurus tunnels.

Against cold silence, listen for the bird's reassuring song, the rhythms
of axe chipping tight-lipped stone, your own quickened step.

Finally, breathless, climb back to the fresh air of an easy chair,
slip your hand into a soiled pocket, finger the payload:

perhaps, a shiny nugget,
perhaps, a lovely lump of coal.

perhaps, a shiny nugget,
    perhaps, a lovely lump of coal.

LEFT, TRAIN OF THOUGHT, 2011. RIGHT, ENDLESS TRAIN, 2011.

Train of Thought

Endlesstrain, Endlesstrain,
engine far, far down the track.

Your echoing whistle screams
decades beyond the vanishing point.

On and on you haul
thought-coupled-to-thought

across miles of mind, never stopping.
Not for freight or coal

or station house. Not for this hobo
scrabbling aboard, stumbling off,

repeatedly. At night your baggage
cars stream on through dreams

then barrel out the dark tunnel,
seamless into morning.

But I've decided:
I WILL NOT RIDE TODAY.

Old compulsion pulls me toward
the tracks where spray-paint graffiti

shouts my name, familiar passengers
beg attention. Just observe, I say,

easing back onto the platform.
Clackety boxcars and tankers

disappear, give way to
random pullmans and flatcars.

You barrel on.
I do not climb aboard.

Onlythoughts.
Onlythoughts.

From the caboose a signalman
waves a silent lantern.

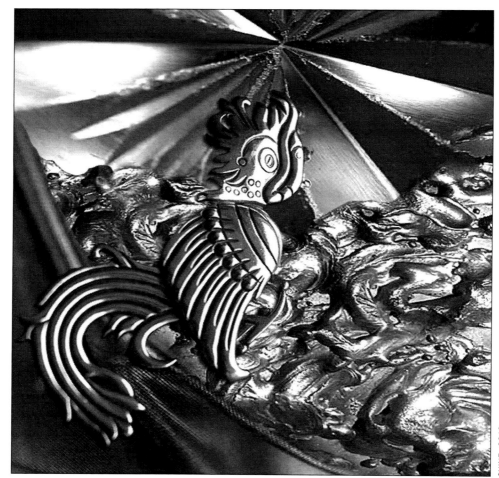

SHINE, 2010.

Reflections on Gray

I celebrate gray:
the pointy-head crayon standing
tall and proud in a first-grader's
box of used-up yellows and blues
and peeled purple nubs.

I celebrate gray: the first
prominent hair to stand out
from its plain brown neighbors
on a middle-aged head.

I extol the understated beauty
of wolf and whale, old ashen
faces, gravel wedged in my tire
tread, the soft melding sameness
of overcast sky and ocean.

Above all, I applaud
dull moon-rock, devoid of Mars'
spanking red dust and our
planet's cheerful greenery.
This plain gray ball circling Earth
whispers nightly its waxing,
waning, universal secret:

*The difference between
gray and silver is Shine.*

Can you hear him? *The difference
between gray and silver is Shine!*

When I deciphered the moonbeam
message, I began to pan my streams,
chisel my shafts and search
city streets for gems of gray,
just to set myself ablaze like
a newborn star and watch their
dullness glow from my burning.

For dingy skies, for smoke and mist
and rain, for pain's dark melancholy
and the hoary head of age, I fuel
and stoke my heart to raging flame,
consume myself in light, till any
moon in my path becomes a mirror
reflecting a hot, glistening heart.

Now I can see your gray—your sad,
your bored, your dirty gray,
as burnished silver, sparkling tinsel,
shiny foil, honed steel—
bright as all the best fire
dancing within me.

When I shine, you shine.

SEE NO EVIL, 2010. VIEWPOINTS, 2010. LETTING GO, 2011.

Thoughts

LEFT, CLOWNS WATCHING OVER THE WORLD, 2010. RIGHT, BEAUTIFUL GIRLS, 2010.

Just Because

Just because it's today.
Just because a sun
I never touched
touched me,

and a sky I couldn't hold
held me,

and a love I didn't understand
understood me.

Just because
the sun
and sky
and love
are free,

I rejoice.

Arc of a Smile

The words stand up straight,
hard-line level. Syntax
upright. Yet the foundation
of this perpendicular
conversation tilts
on the simple arc of a smile,

every rigid word rolling
off the edges of my
cambered heart

like water spilling from
downy wings,
or curvy hips
in spandex suits.

DESERT MIRAGE, 2010.

32

Deserts Happen

Twenty-five degrees
either side of the equator,
and sometimes here
in my head,
deserts happen.

They say the vast Sahara,
more than once, lived as a sea.
More than once,
withered to lake and marsh
then drained dead dry,
leaving wave and ripple
of wind-blown sand
to re-enact vanished waters.

And more than once
encroaching sand and baking sun
and breathless wind
have stolen my ocean of thought.

Streams of words dry up,
lose more moisture than
isolated sprinkles of inspiration
can replace. Flowery thoughts
give way to cactus or creosote.
Lizards and rattlers slither in.

Deserts happen

and sand sifts imperceptibly
down my parched hourglass as
I scan the three-sixty horizon
of gritty sameness
like a hump-back camel
tapping reserves
and instincts for the next oasis.

In the distance
the fragrance of rain.

In the distance
the fragrance of rain

EYE CONTACT, 2009.

the unspoken conversation
of eyes

Eye Contact

A smiling waitress clears fries
and forks, and after a while, kindly
stops stopping at our table.

We linger over ice cream in
sweaty glasses, and slow sips
of ordinary words accompanied by
the unspoken conversation of eyes.

Your comfortable gaze sees
through me, sees all of me, while
I search your deep blues like an
unabridged dictionary,
turning page after page,
reading back to you inadequate
definitions for our love.

The restaurant empties, and still
we sit, fingers meeting on Formica,

your thumb absently stroking
the length of mine,
eyes laughing.

At the counter where you pay
the bill, a cook in a white apron
turns, asks if we are newlyweds.
Newlywed for more than
thirty years, you say.

Now, one empty plate,
a single fork, sit on the table
by my sofa. I make space
on my lap for the cat,
pretend he is listening to me,
purring gentle response.

My eyes smile
with unspoken words.

WEIGHT OF THOUGHTS, 2011.

The Weight of Thought

Heavy. So heavy, this cannon-ball head,
this blood like mercury sludging my veins. Heavy,
the sated stomach, the twenty-foot coil of gut
with its undigested load of lead.

How can these granite legs,
these ponderous elephant legs, move an inch
on a day when one dark cloud outweighs a mountain?

And how can the next delicate wisp of thought
blow that cumbersome cloud off course,
sweep me up again. Light. So light,
my cellophane skin, my tissue-paper bones,
my heart a blissful mote of dust, floating.

my cellophane skin,
my tissue-paper bones...floating

FIERY THOUGHT, 2010.

Incinerated Thought

I sit at my heart's blaze
to burn the brittle yellow story,
to torch the outworn narrative,
every exhausted scene:

hero and victim together
turning to red-gold flame
and wisp of smoke,

the story within the story
bursting into brilliant sparks
quenched by capacious sky,

the last scattered handful of
ashen commentary sifting
dust thin over soil and stone.

I rise
light as the drifting smoke
of incinerated thought.

What We Love

Somewhere a young monk
in saffron robes clutches his one
clay bowl, and a village boy
rolls up his grass-mat bed,
while my teenage son wrestles
the overwhelment of a middle-class
garage with its two motorcycles,
two cars, too little work space.

He edges a sedan a few feet back,
the open driver's door catching
his dad's prize cycle. A lunge
to save the bike leaves the auto
rolling till it meets his father's car,
parked close behind in the driveway:

a three-vehicle accident
without leaving the garage.

These men I love exchange
testosteroned words: son bolts,

husband fumes, leaving me
alone, sitting in tear-streaked
frustration on the fireplace hearth,
pressed thin beneath the weight of
every excess. A thought lifts me

suddenly outside myself, beyond
the yard, onto the asphalt street.
I watch my home engulfed in flame,
a fire-hose wetting the last ash
of its million possessions, until

cars and chairs and chotskies,
begging bowls, mats, and words
seem to matter not at all. They are
smoke and cinder, compared

to the grand excess spilling
from my emptied heart—
full again with love
for two disquieted men.

a three-vehicle accident
without leaving the garage

AWE, 2010.

40

Stand in Awe

A flower-crested casket rested
a few feet from the front pew
where the widow sat in black

crumpled smallness, pressed left
and right and deep behind by
hundreds of voices singing

about peace like a river. And she
was swept away in the flood of it,
the rushing immensity

of a moment spilling its banks.
What was there to do, but
close her eyes and stand—

face upturned, arms uplifted,
hands opened wide, all
of her withered heart stretched

into the only gesture big enough
to hold the whole of comfort
and surrender.

Reverent Heart

Pay attention to the dance
of dust as it worships
in a shaft of light,
to hymns of wind
and housefly wings,
soup-pot incense,
asphalt altars.

Revere the symmetry
of pine groves and
fence posts,
little girls holding hands,
book spines lining shelves.

At the holy commotion
of playground, the liturgy
of marketplace, bare your
head. And bend the knee
to sacred rainbows
shining from horizons
and puddles and fish scales.

For mountains and anthills,
for galaxies and grains of
sand, stand in awe.
Always stand in awe.

42

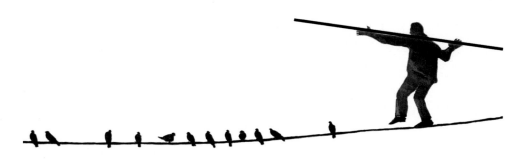

Awkward

Do you ever wonder why
love can be so awkward?
All the other
beautiful things
are graceful and elegant
and happily timed.
But love,
the most beautiful of all,
has no words
and two left feet.

Delicate Balance

On this seesaw, you
balance a hundred frowns
with your smile,

a thousand fears
with joyful expectation,
a million tears
with your laughter.

You walk a thin cable
high above ordinary life
holding a tipped pole
six-men wide.

This off-kilter world
might hurl out of orbit
without the delicate balance
of your happy soul.

TIME ENOUGH, 2011.

Time Enough

All the sixties
tick into twenty-fours
and another will be gone
before long. But

if you start now,
there is time enough
to look for
beautiful things.

If you start now,
there is time.

If you
start now,
there is
time.

Retirement Accounts

Held in lifetime escrow:
wishes for a fifteen-minute break.
Half-hour nap. Unscheduled day.
Leisurely weekend. Long vacation.

Time to read a novel,
sprawl limp in a lawn chair,
have an uninterrupted night,
meal, conversation, thought.

Held in trust: this million wishes
for time, more time, enough time,
all waiting for fine-print conditions
of productive life
to be met in full. Finally,

comes the lump-sum payment
of accumulated deposits,
the pot of minutes
at the end of a six-decade rainbow.

Within a month I open
a new account,
deposit in escrow a thousand wishes
for new things to do
with TIME.

FREESTYLE, 2011. SUNRISE DANCE, 2010. RIBBON DANCE, 2010.

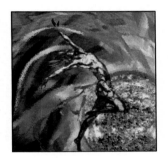

My Dance

No Pale Moon

You were no
pale morning moon
reflection
of a distant fire

no lifeless ball
circling round
another circling ball

You were a dazzling
radiant star
white light
red heat
destined to
extravagant
explosion

Some speck
of your last dust
shot across
my darkened sky
and burst
into a wish

Supermoon

Deep night, I wake startled
to a room lit by flames of moonlight
scorching the walls, a campfire glow
burning my bed.

Curling back toward dusky sleep,
thoughts drift like smoke
through moon-bright scenes:

thin soles of hobo shoes
tapping rhythms of night songs
against glinting steel rails
and timber ties. Dark feet

of ancient nomads dancing across
cooled sand, wide eyes worshipping
the god of the perigee moon
regally posed on the duned horizon.

A woman, perhaps me, splashing
in a river of light.

me,
splashing
in a river
of light

An extreme supermoon, like that of March 19, 2011, occurs about every eighteen years, when
a moon is its fullest and also at its lowest perigee (closest point to Earth). It appears as much
as 14% wider and 30% brighter than other full moons.

UNTAMED, 2011.

50

Caged Wildness

The danger of
dark forests and
untamed creatures

is their siren call
to the caged wildness
of my heart.

Falling prey
to their cunning
is nothing

compared to
the danger
of not

dancing
wild
to their
song.

Sight of Soaring

Because the sight of soaring
untethers my feral heart,
any wide-winged bird will do.

Let binoculared watchers
clutching *Sibley Guides*
travel far to sight rare fowl

while my soul
leaps from nearby tree tops,
rises from highway carrion

to glide the thermals
for miles, for hours
alongside common vultures,

our featherless faces
sun-streaked,
our lame feet
skimming a sky-blue floor.

FREESTYLE, 2011.

Spine Dance

No straight-back Riverdance tonight.
No ballroom posture,
no shoulder frame. This dance is a coiled
cobra rising from my sacral basket,
climbing my notched bones to find the flute.

My helpless skull,
my effortless elbows and wrists,
these thighs, knees, toes all follow
the serpent lead, all flow like streams from
the fountain of two dozen vertebrae.

Soft eyes sweep ceiling, then floor,
every surface of this turning room,
this whirling universe. I rise and
fall in waves, swell, crest, spill—moved
by wind shifting along my inner ridge.

The music ends, the cobra coils
back into the dark, but all night long I hear

his love song
to the lovely spine.

LEFT, RIBBON DANCE, 2011.

stripped down
*   to Superman tights,*
the phone-booth door wide open

Superdance

Across the hardwood floor
a small unbuttoned smile

rumples into laughter,
slips off a shoulder,

drops into trampled heaps
beneath rhythm's bare feet.

I whirl wild
on empty boards,

soar alone in endless space,
until the music stops

and I find myself
smiling at a crowd

of open eyes—
my Clark Kent life

stripped down
to Superman tights,

the phone-booth door
wide open.

WAY SHE MOVES, 2011.

Body Dance

HEAD
Like wispy tendrils
of pink Prairie Smoke
blown by north wind,
like dark waves
of starling wings
dipping free-form
across bare sky,
her hair flies wild
around her
dancing head.

HANDS
Unfisted, unfolded,
unable to hold
old secrets,
her hands are at
the mercy of reckless
shoulders and elbows—
that rowdy crowd of
movers and shakers
that fling the fringe
of fingers, snap them
sharp against the wind,
leave them pointing at
the heart of everything.

56

HIPS

In the brief moments
of a single song,
the round, voluptuous hip,
lifting, dropping its soft curves,
speeds a century
of slow-rising suns,
arching, sinking into sunsets.

Then, in reply to
the insistent question mark
of spine, hips spit
staccato answers,
thrust the startled muscle
to birth some newborn dream
screaming into life.

LEGS

The long bones,
femur and tibia,
fold/unfold at oiled hinges,
knees pointing the path

from where she is
to where she will be.

FEET

Her full weight pivots on
twenty-six slender foot-bones,
piercing the dance floor,
driving roots through
soiled layers of history into
deep rivers that rush up
her straight trunk,
drench the spread
of hollow limbs, once again
ready to sprout leaves
and cradle nests of birds.

She sways,
fiercely grounded, until
the next wind shakes her loose,
rips her rooted toes,
turns outstretched branches
into airborne wings.

For an instant,
all of Earth's air,
all the space of spinning
galaxies becomes
her home.

MESSAGE IN A BOTTLE, 2011. SPEAK PEACE, 2011. MY SEASONS, 2011.

Out loud

LEFT, WALLS TALK, 2010. RIGHT, JOY RIDE, 2011.

Joy Ride

Before effort and edit—
while my first two-wheeler's
rubber tires and my fine hair
and the welling tears of self-awe

flew together down
a tar-and-gravel street—

I knew only that poems
erupting from within
felt oh! so beautiful,
rhythm catching cadence
of pedal and chain

rhymes hanging in autumn air
like lines from radio songs
and Sunday hymns.

Before number-two pencils,
before affirming breve and ictus
of scansion—poetry rode tandem
on handlebars and scattered
weightless into iambic clouds,

no audience
but the wind.

BEYOND RAIN, 2011.

beyond the indigo
downpour

Torrential Talk

I stand bone-soaked
in a sudden word storm,
pelted by torrents
of dark thunderous talk
whirling from every
direction. Mouths roar,
tongues spit bolts of lightning,
thirty-mile-an-hour breath
hammers my back.

Then you invite me to step
into the quiet shelter
of your blue umbrella eyes.

A patch of pale sky
opens unexpectedly
beyond the indigo downpour.

Passing Storms

Last night the sky cried—
her heaving sobs
uprooting ancient trees,
her sudden wailing tears
covering curbs, flooding
every open space.

I wept with her,
together draining
our black
and noisy clouds.

Then, spent,
we both fell silent
and moved on,
the sun rising in our wake.

MESSAGE IN A BOTTLE, 2011.

64

Talking Out Loud

No, no, she didn't pack The Question
in her travel bag. Perhaps she left it
on a bed-side table. Or in the pocket
of a shirt now agitating in the washer
along with mismatched imperatives.

For this downstream rush of words,
which might picnic indefinitely
on a sandbar or spill into a wide river
or an ocean, it's enough that she
brought thoughts ending with. . .
ellipses.

As conversation flows along,
drifting off course here, jammed
on a rock there, interrupted by the
splash of a sunning turtle, she will

unexpectedly hear her own voice speak
a Perfect Answer. Then she'll see, washed
up on her beach, that puzzling Question
she had tucked into a bottle and tossed
into her own deep sea.

I Wait for Words

I drink from a trickle
at the surface

imagining the stream
that tumbles
underground

mysterious caverns
with deep pools
of thought

internal dialogues
dashed against
purifying rocks

an unexpected
stone bank
turning flow to flood.

I wait for words
to pour from your lips.

LISTEN CLOSELY, 2010.

Beneath the Noise

Undressing day noise,
I shed octaves and decibels
like rumpled shirts and dirty socks
tossed into a hamper.

Stripped clean, I slip beneath
the silent blanket of night
only to find
those hushed songs
that play unheard all day
suddenly amped up.

Wires hum behind walls,
water sways in earth-packed pipes.
Breath and blood dance
beneath skin,
and synapse to synapse
my thoughts leap like Baryshnikov.

Life's tiniest rhythms,
particle to wave, wave to particle,
thrum in my cells,
lullaby my weary ears to sleep.

From the roof, a multi-lingual
mockingbird announces morning
and another day dresses itself
in layers of silk and denim sound.

Drops of water rush together,
flush, splash, pour, drain.
Spoons scrape bowls.

The city jerks from flat line
to spiking decibels of voice
and radio and lawn mowers,
angry horns and grinding gears.

But now. . .
beneath the noise I hear
the whispered song
of spinning atoms.

Beneath the work-day's
loud coat,
I wear the quiet music.

STORY TELLING, 2009.

68

Weaving the Stories

At the end of his life,
William crosses the river
on a bi-state bus, gets off
at its last stop, 62nd Street.
He is a stranger
to his grandchildren
when he knocks at our door,
and soon after, a stranger
in a casket—they say he owned
a bakery once and played
the mandolin.

Grandpa George lives next door,
watches wrestling
on a round-screen Zenith,
smokes a pipe, dies without
mentioning that he raised mules
on an island
in the Mississippi River,
drove across to St. Louis once
when the muddy water froze.

Beneath a rack of mail-order
double-knit pants and next to the
half-dozen disguised security files
and tidy boxes of oxfords
with perfectly matching purses is
The Suitcase: Mother's suitcase,
protecting its treasure of unsorted
glossy rectangles, each, presumably,
worth a thousand words.

Four sisters and assorted relatives
gather at long tables heaped
with family photographs,
spend a day weaving scattered bits
of history into stories about
a generation that ended
with Mother. I notice an odd series:
me in a red jacket,
a blue or white or turquoise
sweater, me with contacts
or owl-eyed glasses,
curly or straight hair,
always in the same pose
side by side with Mother
while The Suitcase and the stories
I never thought to ask about
sit in the safe, silent company
of oxfords and elastic-waist pants.

MY BIG BROTHER, 2011.

Big Brother

Lined up. Evenly spaced. Nearly perfect.
That's how a paper basket
assembled with white paste
should be. How the one fashioned
by my first-grade hands was not.

And once a hot tear touched it,
the stained construction was less perfect,
the tears less containable.
I told my teacher I was sick.
She called for my brother
who left his sixth-grade class
to walk me home,
my steps quick against his long stride,
my narrow shoulders bobbing
beside his narrow waist.

I never mentioned the basket.
Never abandoned my delight in the beauty
of things aligned and properly spaced.
Never stopped loving my big brother,
so tall, so nearly perfect.

SPEAK PEACE, 2011

Battle Lines

It's in the breadth of a nose
slant of eye
pigment of skin

Serb and Muslim
Hutu, Tutsi. Aryan, Jew
red and yellow, black and white

It's in the bend of the knee
words of the Book
blood in the veins

Isaac and Ishmael
Crusade, Inquisition
Jihad, Seisen, Reconquista

It's in the edge of a river
the wall of a city
a tree or stone set in the field

Alexander, Napoleon, Adolf
Persian, Roman, Mongol, Ming

Looking down
Looking away

It's in every hairbreadth line
we draw

Peace Pipe

In the curling wisp
of a moment
I know there is

no enemy
no weapon or war paint
no battle in my heart

The only howling dance
left to circle the fire—
a celebration of Light

What You Have

Seeds. Sadness.
Manure.
The common cold.
Prosperity
or poverty.
Fear. Gossip.
Love. Joy.

Whatever you have,
you can spread.

AWE, 2010, TSUNAMI WAVES, 2011. INEVITABLE, 2010.

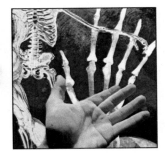

goodbyes

LEFT, EARTHWORMS, 2009.   RIGHT, FISHING TOGETHER.

Earthworms

It happens the first week of March,
perhaps the second,
after a spring rain washes up
a wave of earthworms
from their sea of dark soil
onto the asphalt beach
of my driveway.

Suddenly weeping,
I sweep away
their too-soon withered remains,
along with a surfaced memory:

My father's strong hands
lifting a pitchfork of damp earth,

waiting for his little girl's
tentative fingers
to pull out wriggling worms,
drop them in his fishing pail.

RUSSELL, IRMA, KATHY.

It happens on an almost-spring
day when a gray sky blows in
a cloud of unexpected sadness,
sweeping me grave-side

where strong hands, too soon,
carry a casket to a plot
of freshly turned earth.

RUSSELL LOHRUM, 10.17.17—3.10.83

ELEPHANT MOURNS, 2010.

78

The Weight of Bones

The elephant mourns, brings branches to cover
a motionless body, heaved back to dust.

Tight in the curl of her trunk she carries away
a shard of ivory as she moves with the cowherd

down paths pressed by one less set of footprints.
Who knows how long the elephant remembers,

how long she grieves, believes that her happiness
lies, irretrievable, beneath the weight

of bleached bones and bramble. Perhaps in sleepless
nights she watches old stories acted endlessly against

the dark curtain of sky—memory's single spotlight
casting larger-than-life shadows, till finally

the painful clamor of recall gives way to softer sounds:
her own fresh footfall on the path, surprising echoes of joy.

surprising echoes
of joy

TSUNAMI WAVES, 2011., RIGHT, MY SEASONS, 2011.

80

My Tsunami

The turnings are slight
and pale now,
like green draining
from October leaves,

Ontario winds sagging into
the last edge of southern heat,
our portrait smiles fading

imperceptibly. Your leaving
was an earthquake in my
ocean floor, heaving

tsunami waves that blasted
all ordinary life, drowned me
again and again, then settled

back as though debris on my
shore were mere coincidence.
But the turnings are slight

and pale now: gray drifting
into a blue sky,
tears raining softly, passing.

Marking Time

Mark the time
in bark and limbs:
a zigzag of spindly pines
we planted—
now thick and thirty-foot tall.

Count in flowers:
blossoms of Bradford pear,
dogwood, red bud—
planted in your memory.

Count by seasons of leaves:
pale buds, dense greens,
fiery maples,
then beautiful bits of life
settling gently home,
dust to dust returning.

JILLIAN AT ELEVEN, 2009.

Granddaughters

In one synchronized motion
this suddenly taller child
lifts her eyebrows
and shoulders,
drops them, turns away,
leaving me to wonder:

Was there a moment
when my grandmother
set aside a bowl of flour
or the yellow-handled broom

to press her face hard
into a cotton apron
and choke back tears

because I answered her
in monosyllables,
shrugged off familiar pastimes,

grew up too soon.

Soil of Generations

In a blink of
spring,
crocus gives way to daffodil,
forsythia to lilac.

In a blink,
mother gives way to daughter,
daughter to grandchild.

In their ceaseless cycles
flowers and women
bloom, fade,

bury their lovely seeds
in the soil of generations,

preparing always
for the next spring.

JILLIAN AT THIRTEEN, 2011.

LETTING GO, 2010.

84

Evolution of Letting Go

The old man watches
a tiny frog
with new-formed legs
letting go the tadpole safety
of dark water
for a bright-lit bank.

Long ago, he let go
a safe hand
to wobble his first steps,
let go the crib rails
to wander wider rooms.

He let go homestead,
home town,
parents for partner,
one job for the next,

a thousand good ideas
for a thousand better.

Now the old man sits
pond-edge, watches
the red-and-white bobber
of his fishing line float
like a planet
in rippled stillness.

He feels his damp cotton shirt
rise and fall to slow breathing,
wonders when one breath
will not be followed
by another:

the last letting go.

let go the crib rails
to wander wider rooms

INEVITABLE, 2009.

A Bit of Sadness

A twinge of sadness
for the solitary winter tree
that failed to green
this spring, a bit for
wayward earthworms
shriveled on the walkway,

for faded blossom
and fallen leaf,
for turtle shells
left spinning on the road.

Before life trained me
to stand in line at
man-made mortuaries,
to pull aside for solemn
hearse processions,

I was a happy child
who played games
with budless branches
and romped through
nature's casual deaths.
I did not know
one bit of sadness
for life moving on.

My Seasons

Two pale-green decades
of limber shoot unfolding,
stretching skyward,
lean and windblown
in mottled shade of family canopy.

A pair of glossy, frenzied decades,
sturdy limbs claiming their own
space, toiling every sunlit moment,
turning light to leaf. Then decades

of letting go, shedding
the emerald mask to reveal
deep red and glistening gold,
finally tossing even those last
trinkets to the wind. Now this:

thick, deep rooted decades,
my bared frame, its storied scars,
its initials carved in heart shapes,
clear at last against a vast horizon,
my old treasures tucked inside,
ring within ring,

unafraid of axe blade
or blaze of an unknown hearth.

DECADES, 2011.

The Last Yellow Pencil

When I'm gone, dear ones, find among the things
I'll never need again, a yellow pencil from piles
in office or bedside or kitchen drawers.

While you arrange to wrap up my good life,
keep that pencil in your pocket and let its tiny point
remind you to strike out the word "should"
from every conversation. Let there be no
"we should" in your farewell plans.
This party is for you, not me.

Burn my bones or bury them, as it pleases you.
I won't care. Play the tunes you like. Invite the folks
who make you happy and let the rest nod at my obit.

And don't forget to flip my last yellow pencil
to the pink rubber end now and then
to erase "too soon" from all dialog.

If I die tonight, my dears, or live to an auspicious age,
it will be long enough
for me to edit out all but the best,
and time for you to do the same.

KATHY, KEYHOLE HOUSE, 2009.